CONTENTS

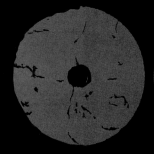

WELCOME TO THE WORLD OF INFOGRAPHICS

Using icons, graphics and pictograms, infographics visualise information in a whole new way!

SEE HOW MUCH SEA LEVELS FELL DURING THE ICE AGES.

FIND OUT HOW EARLY HUMANS CAUGHT AND KILLED THEIR FOOD.

SEE HOW BIG A SABRE-TOOTHED TIGER'S FANGS GREW.

READ ABOUT WHEN THE EARLIEST HUMAN ANCESTORS EVOLVED.

COMPARE THE SIZE OF HUGE ANIMALS FROM THE STONE AGE.

WHAT WAS THE STONE AGE?

The Stone Age was the earliest and longest period of human culture. It started about 2.6 million years ago (MYA) when our human ancestors began to use and make stone tools. The period lasted for more than 2 million years, finishing when humans started to work with metal, about 4,000 years ago.

OLD STONE AGE

2.6 MILLION YEARS AGO (MYA)

PALAEOLITHIC

THE OLD STONE AGE – 2.6 MILLION TO 10,000 YEARS AGO

2.6 MYA
THE FIRST SIMPLE STONE TOOLS ARE MADE

1.5 MYA
EVOLUTION OF *HOMO ERECTUS*

800,000 YEARS AGO
EARLY HUMANS START TO USE FIRE TO COOK, WARM THEMSELVES AND SCARE OFF PREDATORS

800,000–200,000 YEARS AGO
HUMAN BRAIN SIZE INCREASES RAPIDLY

The Stone Age accounts for 99 PER CENT of all human history.

NEOLITHIC

THE NEW STONE AGE – 6,000 TO ABOUT 4,000 YEARS AGO

NEW STONE AGE

4,000 YEARS AGO

MIDDLE STONE AGE

MESOLITHIC

THE MIDDLE STONE AGE – 10,000 TO 6,000 YEARS AGO

6,000 YEARS AGO

10,000 YEARS AGO

200,000 YEARS AGO
EVOLUTION OF *HOMO SAPIENS*

TOOL USE

Hominids are the great apes, including humans and extinct human ancestors. The *Homo* group were some of the first hominids to shape and use tools. One of the earliest examples found dates from about 2.6 million years ago, and is a pebble chopper.

18,000 YEARS AGO
HEIGHT OF THE LAST ICE AGE

15,000 YEARS AGO
HUMANS START TO CONTROL AND BREED CERTAIN SPECIES OF ANIMALS AND PLANTS

A pebble chopper is a cutting tool made by chipping off flakes of stone to create a sharp edge.

WHO'S WHO OF THE STONE AGE

The Stone Age saw a surge in the evolution of humans, from the appearance of *Australopithecines*, early people with brains not much larger than apes', to the development of modern humans, *Homo sapiens*.

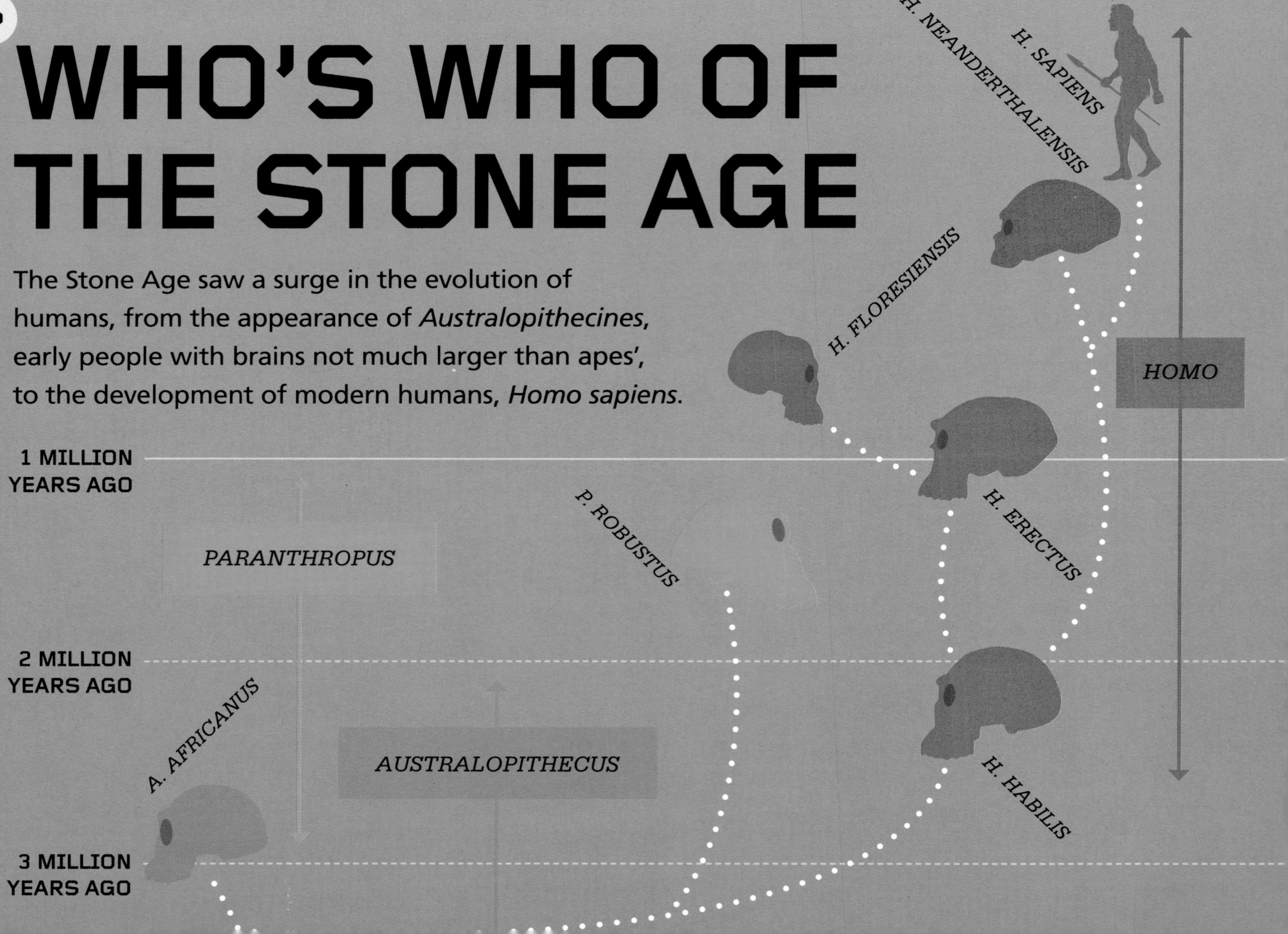

HOMO

AUSTRALOPITHECUS

PARANTHROPUS

H. SAPIENS

H. NEANDERTHALENSIS

H. FLORESIENSIS

H. ERECTUS

H. HABILIS

P. ROBUSTUS

A. AFRICANUS

1 MILLION YEARS AGO

2 MILLION YEARS AGO

3 MILLION YEARS AGO

EARLIEST RELATIVE

The earliest fossils of human relatives date back nearly 7 million years, far before the Stone Age, and are from a species known as *Sahelanthropus tchadensis*. By the start of the Stone Age, around 2.5 million years ago, several more human-like species developed in two groups known as *Australopithecus* and *Paranthropus*. Modern humans' direct ancestors, the *Homo* group, first appeared about 2.8 million years ago.

SAHELANTHROPUS TCHADENSIS SKULL

BRAIN SIZE

As various groups of early hominids evolved, their brain capacity grew bigger and bigger, a sign that the species were becoming more and more intelligent.

4–500 ML
INTERNAL SKULL VOLUME

AUSTRALOPITHECUS AFARENSIS

600 ML
INTERNAL SKULL VOLUME

HOMO ERECTUS

1,200 ML
INTERNAL SKULL VOLUME

HOMO SAPIENS

SAHELANTHROPUS TCHADENSIS

EARLY HOMINIDS

4 MILLION YEARS AGO

5 MILLION YEARS AGO

6 MILLION YEARS AGO

BRAINY SPECIES

The name *Homo sapiens* is Latin for 'wise man'. *Homo sapiens* first evolved in Africa about 200,000 years ago.

ON THE MOVE

After humans evolved in Africa, they took more than 100,000 years to spread out of the continent. But when they did, they moved rapidly, populating every part of the globe in less than 100,000 years and replacing other hominid species that had spread before them.

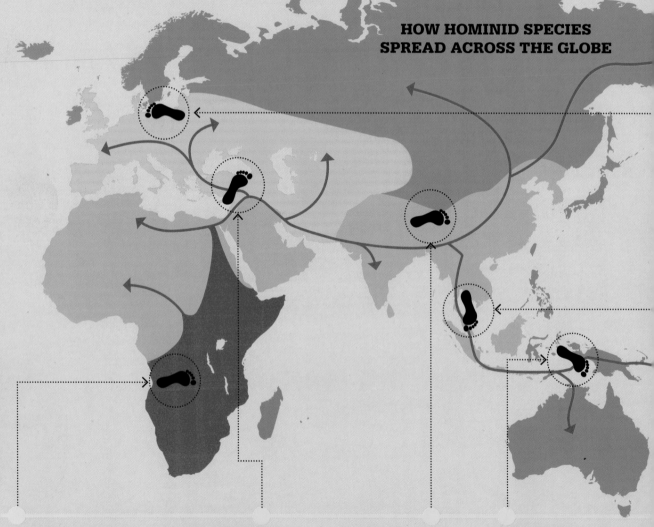

HOW HOMINID SPECIES SPREAD ACROSS THE GLOBE

ABOUT 200,000 YEARS AGO
Modern humans evolved in Africa

ABOUT 75,000 YEARS AGO
Homo sapiens left Africa

ABOUT 50,000 YEARS AGO
Humans reached southern Asia

ABOUT 46,000 YEARS AGO
A land bridge allowed humans to reach Australia

HOMO
NEANDERTHALENSIS

HOMO
ERECTUS

HOMO
SAPIENS

1.1 METRES

SPREAD OF HOMINID SPECIES

HOMO NEANDERTHALENSIS

HOMO ERECTUS

HOMO SAPIENS

HOMO FLORESIENSIS

One species of early human, *Homo floresiensis*, survived until about 50,000 years ago. They were just 1.1 metres tall and remains have only been found on the island of Flores, Indonesia.

ABOUT 43,000 YEARS AGO
Homo sapiens arrived in Europe

ABOUT 30,000 YEARS AGO
The islands of eastern Asia were reached

ABOUT 14,500 YEARS AGO
Humans cross a land bridge into North America

ABOUT 1,000 YEARS AGO
Humans spread throughout the Pacific islands, arriving in New Zealand last

USING TOOLS

HAMMERSTONE
Used to smash stone cores to produce sharp flakes.

The Stone Age saw a massive change in how humans used tools. While early Stone Age tools were little more than clumsily shaped stones, tools from the end of the Stone Age were precisely made, allowing the user to carry out intricate work.

Shaping and sharpening
Tools became more intricate, with complicated handaxes and even more delicate flake tools made. Stones were also shaped into sharp points that could be fixed to a long stick to make a spear.

AWLS
Very sharp, thin points used to make holes in materials, such as skins, so they could be sewn together to make clothing.

NEEDLES
Often made from bone and used to sew clothing together.

Delicate tools
Tools from the later stages of the Stone Age were very intricate and used a range of materials, including bone, ivory and antler.

BETWEEN ABOUT 30,000 AND 23,000 YEARS AGO

STONE CORE
Flakes were chipped off to produce a sharp edge to cut meat and to extract bone marrow.

STONE FLAKES
Small, sharp flakes were used for delicate cutting work.

FIRST TOOLMAKERS
Homo habilis was the first species of hominid to make tools. The name *Homo habilis* means 'skilled man'.

POINT
Used to make spears and darts to attack fast-moving prey or ward off dangerous predators.

BETWEEN 400,000 AND 200,000 YEARS AGO

USING FIRE
Scientists have found evidence dating from more than 70,000 years ago that early humans were using fire to heat stones. Heating the stones made them easier to shape into tools.

HARPOON
Carved from bone, antler or ivory, these had barbs to stop prey, such as fish, wriggling free from the end.

HUNTING AND FISHING

Improvements in Stone Age weapons and tools allowed prehistoric people to catch more and bigger prey. They also developed new ways of catching food, providing them with a good source of protein and other nutrients.

METHODS OF TRAPPING LARGE PREY

Prehistoric hunters would sometimes chase prey until it became too tired to run any more. They would then kill the prey by stabbing it with a spear.

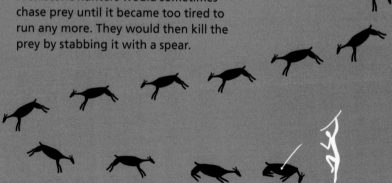

Prey that was too big, such as a mammoth, or too fast could be herded over the edge of a cliff.

HUNTED TO EXTINCTION

Stone Age humans became so good at hunting that they may have driven several species to extinction. This included the *Glyptodon* – an armoured mammal that looked a bit like an armadillo, but was the size of an ox.

1.4 M

68 KILOGRAMS

THE WEIGHT OF SOME PREHISTORIC CATFISH.
IF CAUGHT, ONE COULD SUPPLY ENOUGH MEAT
TO FEED 80 PEOPLE FOR TWO DAYS.

Alternatively, hunters would
target old or sick prey,
which was easier to catch.

800,000

NUMBER OF YEARS AGO
THAT HUMANS LEARNT
HOW TO CONTROL FIRE
AND COOK THE FOOD
THEY CAUGHT AND
GATHERED.

Prey could be herded towards a
swamp where it would become
stuck and could be killed easily.

The oldest known human artefacts are
three wooden spears
found in Germany. They are about
400,000 thousand years old and were
found near the butchered remains of 10 horses.

GATHERING AND GROWING

As well as hunting and catching animals to eat, the first people also gathered wild plants and berries as part of their diet.
By learning how to grow and cultivate certain plants, however, they could produce a more dependable food source and increase the amount available for them to eat.

GATHERING

The range of food that could be gathered depended on where people lived, but it would have included:

CATMINT

RUE

PLANTS
such as dandelions and nettles

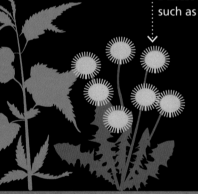

SOME PLANTS, SUCH AS CATMINT AND RUE, MAY HAVE BEEN USED TO PRODUCE EARLY MEDICINES.

DOMESTICATION OF ANIMALS

DOGS FOR HUNTING
15,000–12,000 YEARS AGO

SHEEP, GOATS, CATTLE AND PIGS FOR MEAT, MILK AND SKINS
11,000–9,000 YEARS AGO

OXEN TO PULL EARLY PLOUGHS AND WAGONS
6,000 YEARS AGO

EGGS
from birds' nests

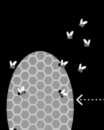

12,000

the number of years ago that humans first learnt to grow simple crops and rear animals. This early form of farming provided prehistoric people with more food than hunting and gathering.

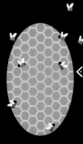

HONEY
from wild beehives

ARD
An early type of plough

FRUIT

NUTS

SIMPLE PLOUGH

The first ploughs were invented about 5,000 years ago. These early farming tools consisted of a long spiked pole that was pulled along by cattle, creating furrows that made it easier to plant seeds.

BERRIES

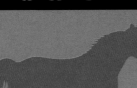

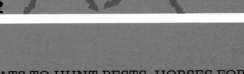

CATS TO HUNT PESTS, HORSES FOR MEAT AND TRANSPORT, SILK MOTHS FOR SILK THREAD AND CLOTH
5,000 YEARS AGO

CAMELS TO CARRY GOODS
5,000–3,500 YEARS AGO

CRAFTS AND TECHNOLOGY

Throughout the Stone Age, human arts and technology went through some huge changes with the creation of items such as wheeled transport, and techniques from music and painting to early mathematics.

HUNTERS

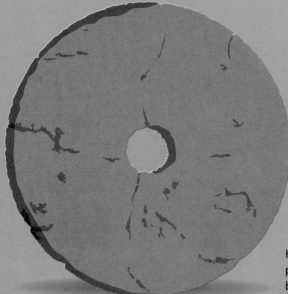

ROUND AND ROUND

The wheel was invented in Mesopotamia, in what is now Iraq, around 3500 BCE. However, the first wheels were used as potters' wheels. It was another 300 years before they were used for transport.

COUNTING STICK

A baboon bone found in the Lebombo Mountains in Swaziland, in Africa, contains the earliest evidence of a human counting above ten. It has 29 marks on it and some scientists believe that it may have been used to keep track of the moon's phases (a lunar month is about 29 days long). The bone is more than 35,000 years old.

ABOUT
11,000
YEARS AGO, STONE AGE PEOPLE DISCOVERED THAT CLAY COULD BE MADE HARDER AND STRONGER BY BAKING IT IN A FIRE RATHER THAN DRYING IT IN THE SUN.

PAINTINGS

Many cave paintings show scenes of hunting, revealing the types of animal that Stone Age people ate, including horses and cattle. Prehistoric animal paintings have been found in Spain, Indonesia and Romania.

HORSE

CATTLE

GOAT

DEER

STONE AGE COLOUR PALETTE

Stone Age paints were made by mixing charcoal, iron oxide rocks (red rocks that are similar to rusted metal) and yellow ochre with spit, water or animal fat to form a paste.

RED OXIDE

YELLOW OCHRE

CHARCOAL

HAND PAINTINGS

Some cave images show the outlines of humans hands. They were made by spraying paint through long straws. These hand patterns have been found in caves in France, Spain, Indonesia and Australia.

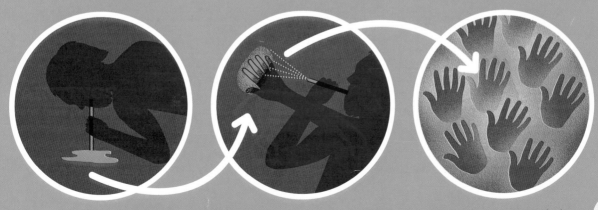

1. Paint sucked into straw   **2.** Paint blown over hand   **3.** Hand silhouette revealed

STONE AGE BUILDINGS

The first Stone Age buildings were temporary structures which early people built with what they could find as they moved from place to place. Once they had learnt to farm the land and rear animals, humans started to build permanent buildings.

2 MILLION

the number of years ago that hominids began building the first shelters. They were arrangements of stones holding tree branches in position.

SOME OF THESE EARLY SHELTERS WERE NEARLY 15 METRES LONG – ABOUT TWICE THE LENGTH OF A LONDON BUS.

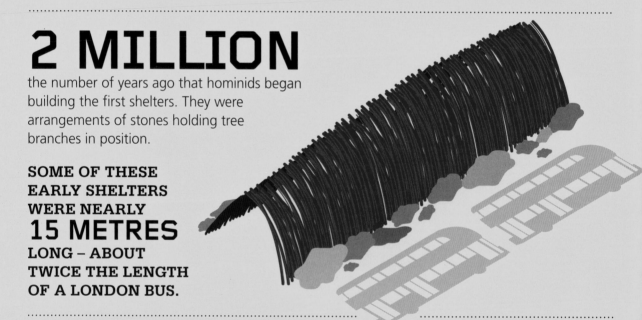

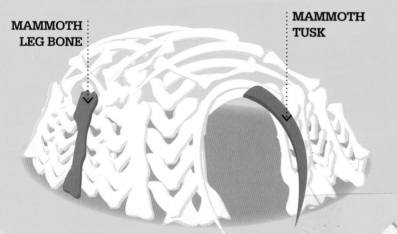

MAMMOTH LEG BONE

MAMMOTH TUSK

149

the number of mammoth bones that were used to make four shelters discovered in the Ukraine. They date from about 15,000 years ago.

STONE DWELLINGS

Two stone buildings known as the Knap of Howar on Orkney, Scotland, date from about 3700 BCE and are some of the oldest surviving stone houses in the world.

TURF ROOF LAID OVER A WOODEN FRAME

STONE WALLS

STONE CIRCLES AND OTHER MONUMENTS

Prehistoric stone circles are found in several parts of the world, including North America, Europe and Africa.

1,300

THE APPROXIMATE NUMBER OF STONE CIRCLES FOUND IN BRITAIN AND IRELAND.

WHAT IS A HENGE?

A henge is a large, circular Stone Age earthwork, consisting of a raised bank and ditch surrounding a flat area. It may contain a monument, such as a stone circle.

FLAT AREA

CIRCULAR DITCH

CIRCULAR RAISED BANK

ONE OF THE LARGEST HENGES CONSTRUCTED IS FOUND AT AVEBURY, UK. IT WAS BUILT AROUND 5,000 YEARS AGO AND MEASURES ABOUT 425 METRES IN DIAMETER. THAT'S MORE THAN FOUR TIMES THE LENGTH OF A FOOTBALL PITCH.

STONEHENGE

The stone circles at Stonehenge were built in stages over a period of nearly 1,500 years. We don't know what they were used for, but some features line up with astronomical events, such as sunrise on the summer solstice, the longest day of the year.

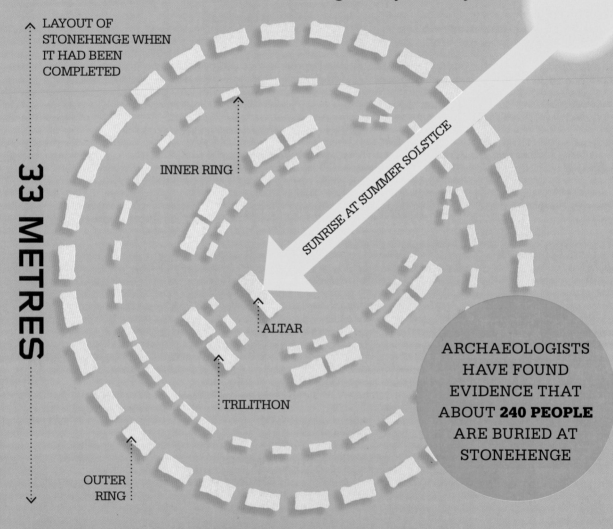

LAYOUT OF STONEHENGE WHEN IT HAD BEEN COMPLETED

33 METRES

INNER RING

SUNRISE AT SUMMER SOLSTICE

ALTAR

TRILITHON

OUTER RING

ARCHAEOLOGISTS HAVE FOUND EVIDENCE THAT ABOUT **240 PEOPLE** ARE BURIED AT STONEHENGE

CONSTRUCTION TIMELINE Stonehenge was constructed in several stages.

(ABOUT) 3000 BCE
The first major works were carried out, with the digging of two circular ditches about 100 metres across.

(ABOUT) 2500 BCE
Huge stones were erected to form an inner horseshoe and an outer circle.

(ABOUT) 2250 BCE
More stones were erected and a long avenue was made, linking the site to the River Avon.

(ABOUT) 1500 BCE
The last construction work involved digging rings of pits around the site.

TWO TYPES OF STONE WERE USED TO BUILD STONEHENGE.

PRESELI HILLS

MARLBOROUGH DOWNS

STONEHENGE

BLUESTONES

were brought from the Preseli Mountains in South Wales up to 240 kilometres away by one of two possible routes. They were dragged on rollers to the Welsh coast, floated on rafts across to England and then dragged on rollers to the site. Each weighed as much as an African elephant.

4 Tonnes

50 Tonnes

SARSEN STONES

weighed as much as 25 cars and were brought from the Marlborough Downs, about 40 kilometres away. They were pulled there on sledges. About 600 men were needed to move each stone. Sarsen is a type of sandstone from southern England.

BUILDING A TRILITHON

Trilithons are arrangements of stones with huge vertical slabs holding up horizontal blocks. Other trilithons can be found on the island of Malta and at the Osirion in Abydos, Egypt.

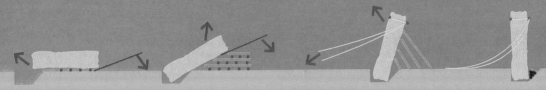

THE VERTICAL SLABS WERE LOWERED INTO PITS AND PULLED UPRIGHT.

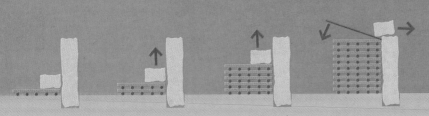

THE HORIZONTAL BLOCKS WERE RAISED USING SCAFFOLDING THAT WAS BUILT UP ONE LAYER AT A TIME, AND THEN PUSHED INTO PLACE.

STONE AGE BURIALS

People from the Stone Age spent a lot of time and effort honouring their dead. They built huge monuments to them and buried them with grave goods which reflected their role and standing.

TURF ROOF

20 METRES

CHAMBERS

STONE WALL

NEWGRANGE

A Neolithic monument built in Ireland around 3000 BCE, Newgrange is a large mound containing a 20-metre-long passageway with a chamber at the far end and three small chambers leading off that. Archaeologists believe it may have been a place to store the dead and prepare their bodies before burial.

CUTAWAY OF A TYPICAL CAIRN

SOIL MOUND

URN

CAIRNS

One common Neolithic burial monument is a cairn. Cairns were large mounds built over graves. Pottery jars, called urns, holding grave goods of jewellery, weapons and other objects, were often buried in the mounds.

GRAVE

SHAMAN BURIALS

Stone Age bodies were often buried in a crouched or curled-up position with a collection of grave goods. The grave of a shaman, or holy person, buried 12,000 years ago in Israel contained:

AN EAGLE WING

THE PELVIS
OF A LEOPARD

A SEVERED
HUMAN FOOT

TWO
MARTEN
SKULLS

50
TORTOISE
SHELLS

LEG BONE FROM A WILD BOAR

TUMULUS

A type of tomb consisting of a large earth mound covering a grave.

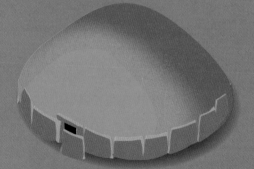

DOLMEN

A structure with two upright megaliths supporting a horizontal stone. Many dolmens were covered with earth and may have been used as tombs.

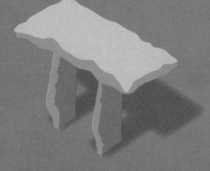

THE ICE AGE

Since the start of the Stone Age, there have been several periods where ice sheets have extended over large parts of the planet, creating cooler periods known as ice ages.

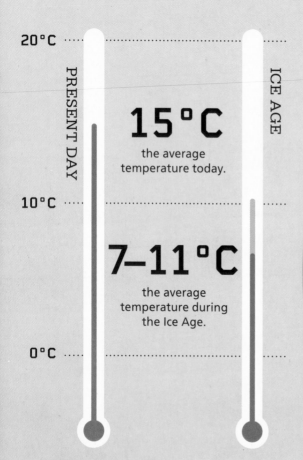

PRESENT DAY

20°C

15°C
the average temperature today.

10°C

7–11°C
the average temperature during the Ice Age.

ICE AGE

0°C

ICE SHEETS
The ice sheets were up to 4 kilometres thick, about two-thirds the height of Kilimanjaro, the tallest mountain in Africa.

KILIMANJARO
5,895 M

4 KILOMETRES

NORTH AMERICA

Ice ages may be caused by changes in the make-up of the atmosphere, variations in the activity of the sun, the eruptions of supervolcanoes and even collisions with objects from outer space.

ICE SHEETS STRETCHED ACROSS MOST OF NORTH AMERICA AND NORTHERN EUROPE

21,000
the number of years ago the last Ice Age started.

120 METRES

LOWEST SEA LEVEL DURING ICE AGE

GREAT PYRAMID
GIZA, 139 M

DROPPING SEA LEVELS

Sea levels dropped by 120 metres – that's almost as tall as the Great Pyramid of Giza. As a result, many landmasses were linked, including the British Isles with mainland Europe and Russia with North America.

ASIA

WOOLLY MAMMOTH

In Europe, ice sheets stretched as far south as Britain and central Germany.

WARMING UP

When the ice sheets retreated and the earth warmed up, more than three-quarters of the large Ice Age mammals died out, including mammoths and sabre-toothed tigers, or smilodons.

SMILODON (SABRE-TOOTHED TIGER)

EUROPE

11,500
the number of years ago the last Ice Age ended.

STONE AGE ANIMALS

Many Stone Age animals were very different to the creatures living today and had evolved to survive the varying conditions during the period. These animals included huge ground sloths, woolly mammals and terrifying sabre-toothed tigers.

MEGATHERIUM
(GIANT GROUND SLOTH)
6 M LONG

Megatherium weighed up to
4 TONNES
about the weight of an African elephant.

SABRE-TOOTHED TIGER
1.2 M

TIGER
95 CM

BIG TEETH ...
The sabre-toothed tiger had two long fangs that measured up to 20 cm long, a little smaller than a basketball.

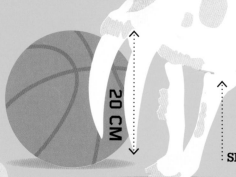

20 CM

SMILODON SKULL

INSULATING LAYERS

To keep them warm in the freezing temperatures, woolly mammoths had coats of fur measuring up to 50 cm long and a layer of fat beneath the skin that was 8 cm thick.

WOOLLY MAMMOTHS DIED OUT AROUND **7,600** YEARS AGO

WOOLLY MAMMOTH
4 M

AFRICAN ELEPHANT
3.3 M

HUMAN 1.6 M

... BIGGER TEETH

A woolly mammoth's tusk could grow to more than

4 metres long – more than twice as long as the height of an adult human. It could weigh more than

90 kilograms about the weight of a kangaroo.

····· UP TO 4 METRES ···········>

WHAT HAPPENED NEXT?

The Stone Age ended in about 3300 BCE when people started to extract metal from rocky ore, known as smelting, and use it to make goods and weapons. The first metals used were copper and bronze, giving this period its name, the Bronze Age.

WHAT IS BRONZE?

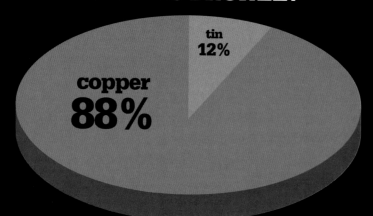

tin
12%

copper
88%

1000 BCE
The approximate date that the Bronze Age ended and was replaced by the Iron Age.

CUNEIFORM

ADVANCING CIVILISATIONS
One of the first Bronze Age civilisations to emerge was Sumer in what is now southern Iraq. It was based around about a dozen city states, including Eridu and Uruk, and developed one of the earliest forms of writing: cuneiform.

SPREAD OF BRONZE AGE

The start of the Bronze Age varied from region to region. It began in the Middle East and Greece before 5000 BCE, but didn't reach Britain until 1900 BCE.

5800–5000 BCE

5000–4000 BCE

4000–3500 BCE

3500–3000 BCE

3000–2500 BCE

2500–2000 BCE

5000 BCE
Bronze Age begins in the Middle East and Greece

SUMER

UR

ZIGGURAT OF UR
Built by Sumerians during the early Bronze Age, in about 2000 BCE.

30 METRES

45 METRES

64 METRES

Ziggurat of Ur

Arc de Triomphe, Paris

29

GLOSSARY

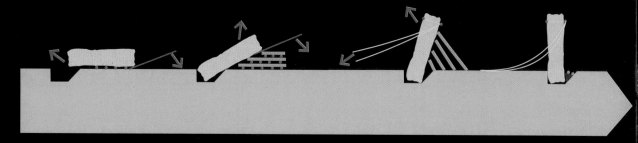

butcher
To kill an animal and slice off its meat to eat.

cairn
A mound of stones or earth used to mark a particular spot and sometimes built over a prehistoric tomb.

dolmen
A Stone Age building that was made up of two vertical stones holding up a horizontal stone, and sometimes used to mark a tomb.

domestication
The control and use of plants and animals as sources of food or to help with hunting, clothing or to carry loads.

extinction
When something has died out and no longer exists.

hammerstone
A large rounded stone that was used to hit other stones and produce sharp edges and tools.

grave goods
Objects that are buried with a dead person in the belief that they will be used in the afterlife.

handaxe
A stone tool that was used for cutting and had one sharp edge and no handle.

henge
A large circular earthwork that usually consisted of a raised bank with a ditch inside it. Within these was a large flat area that often contained a stone circle or wooden posts, which were used for ceremonial purposes.

hominid
A species of animal related to modern humans, *Homo sapiens*. This also includes all the extinct ancestors of modern humans.

ice age
A period of Earth's history when temperatures were lower and large ice sheets spread out from the polar regions.

ice sheet
A thick layer of ice that covers an area for a long period of time.

insulate
To stop or reduce the movement of heat, usually out of the body, keeping it warm.

A strip of land linking two continents.

Mesolithic
A period of the Stone Age. It means 'Middle Stone Age' and relates to the period from about 10,000 years ago to about 6,000 years ago.

Neolithic
A period of the Stone Age. It means 'New Stone Age' and relates to the period from about 6,000 years ago to about 3,300 years ago.

ochre
Natural earth containing minerals that give it a red or yellow colour.

Palaeolithic
A period of the Stone Age. It means 'Old Stone Age' and relates to the period from about 2.5 million years ago to about 10,000 years ago.

plough
A farming tool that is designed to cut and turn soil, preparing it for a crop.

A type of sandstone that is common in parts of southern Britain.

shaman
A tribal wise person or healer.

smelting
Removing metal from a rocky ore usually by using very high temperatures.

species
A group of organisms that share the same physical characteristics and are capable of breeding with one another.

tumulus
Also known as a barrow, this is a mound of earth that has been piled up over a prehistoric tomb or collection of tombs, or even a network of stone burial chambers.

Websites

MORE INFORMATION:
www.bbc.co.uk/guides/ z34djxs
A website with videos and images showing what life was like for people living in the Stone Age.

humanorigins.si.edu
A website from the Smithsonian Institute looking at all aspects of human evolution including what life was like during the Stone Age.

timetravellerkids.co.uk/ time-travel/stone-age/
A fun website packed with facts and information about the Stone Age as well as related crafts and activities that children can do.

MORE GRAPHICS:
www.visualinformation.info
A website that contains a whole host of infographic material on subjects as diverse as natural history, science, sport and computer games.

www.coolinfographics.com
A collection of infographics and data visualisations from other online resources, magazines and newspapers.

www.dailyinfographic.com
A comprehensive collection of infographics on an enormous range of topics that is updated every single day!

INDEX

ACKNOWLEDGEMENTS

First published in Great Britain
in 2016 by Wayland
Copyright © Wayland, 2016
All rights reserved

Editor: Elizabeth Brent
Produced by Tall Tree Ltd
Editor: Jon Richards
Designer: Jonathan Vipond

ISBN: 978 1 5263 0022 5
10 9 8 7 6 5 4 3 2 1

Wayland
An imprint of Hachette
Children's Group
Part of Hodder and Stoughton
Carmelite House
50 Victoria Embankment
London EC4Y 0DZ

An Hachette UK Company
www.hachette.co.uk
www.hachettechildrens.co.uk

Printed and bound in China

The website addresses (URLs) included in this
book were valid at the time of going to press.
However, it is possible that contents or
addresses may have changed since the
publication of this book. No responsibility
for any such changes can be accepted by
either the author or the Publisher.

MIX
Paper from
responsible sources
FSC® C104740

GET THE PICTURE!

Welcome to the world of **infographics!** Icons, pictograms and graphics create an exciting form of data visualisation, presenting information in a new and appealing way.

PLANET EARTH
9780750278461

SPACE
9780750278454

COUNTRIES
9780750283069

MACHINES AND VEHICLES
9780750281287

THE HUMAN BODY
9780750278683

NATURAL RESOURCES
9780750283205

THE HUMAN WORLD
9780750269049

ANIMAL KINGDOM
9780750283199

SPORT
9780750277792

NATURAL WORLD
9780750269032

ART AND ENTERTAINMENT
9780750279628

TECHNOLOGY
9780750283076

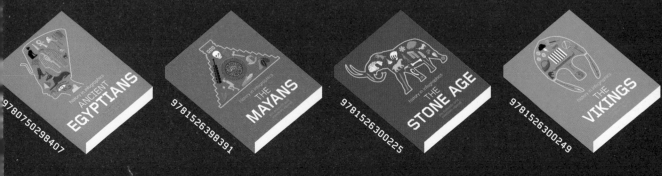

ANCIENT EGYPTIANS
9780750298407

THE MAYANS
9781526398391

THE STONE AGE
9781526300225

THE VIKINGS
9781526300249